# CONVERTIBLE

## REFERRALS

"I've admired, for many years, the way Shaun has honed his system and business building through referrals. The key difference for me is his responsiveness, gratitude, and willingness to help, whether it means direct business for him or not."
—Dan Hughes, Summit Mortgage

"In my eyes Shaun has been a leader in referral marketing for over twenty years. He knows how to consistently build business and help others build their businesses through referrals. Listen to Shaun's valuable insights and apply his techniques and I believe your business will prosper as well."
—Robert Laue, Attorney, Christensen and Laue, P.A.

"Eyes open, ears peeled back to listen, thinking about others first. Sounds simple but very few people live it with the energy and passion the way Shaun has been able to throughout his career. Lots of people talk a good game when it comes to referrals. If you want to learn how to play above the rim, listen to Shaun and implement what he's sharing with you."
—Thomas Barton, CPA

"I've watched Shaun grow his business from zero to a Super Producer. He's always been willing to share but it's great to have the manual now to continue to grow our business to be even stronger."
—Russ Castle, Insurance by Castle

"One of the greatest life lessons I have learned is that it is OK to listen to people who know more than I do about a given subject and run with it! Following Shaun's advice, gleaned from years of outperforming his peers and competitors, will lift you ever closer to your dreams. I stay ahead of the competition by committing to learn successful strategies from great professionals like Shaun Irwin!"
—Mike Stromsoe, *The Unstoppable Profit Producer*

"Shaun's energy and enthusiasm for helping others is contagious. Follow his lead and you'll find people wanting to help you succeed in ways you've only imagined."
—Robert Klas, Jr., Tapemark Company

"In the time I've known Shaun he's always been genuinely interested in people and helping them. Now he's willing to help you too. Listen carefully and implement fanatically so you can jumpstart your life and career."
—Phil Riedel, Atrix International

"Nothing is as satisfying for me as seeing a coaching client succeed. Shaun's done that and more. He's taking something that he's personally gifted at and sharing it with you just like he's shared it countless times with our members. If you're smart, you'll read the book. If you're really smart, you'll start doing what Shaun outlines immediately."
—Michael Jans, President, Agency Revolution

"It's exciting to me that Shaun is releasing this book. When I came to my position I was deeply committed and passionate about the cause but needed leaders to show me how to connect better with the community. Shaun has been an incredible mentor and supporter of me personally and the Cookie Cart's growth and mission."
—Matt Halley, Executive Director, Cookie Cart

"Shaun Irwin understands relationships intuitively better than 95% of the people I meet. Now he's laid it out here for you to understand and take advantage of his expertise. It's my pleasure to be able to tell you to get all you can from this book so your relationships provide dividends for you and others."
—Don Phin, *HR That Works*

"At a time in my life when I was scared and in transition, Shaun armed and mentored me with skills to find my way. It's easy to help people when one sees immediate impact but it's life changing when one helps unconditionally as a part of their DNA. A true servant heart and abundant gratitude are the gifts I hope you'll learn from Shaun."
—Cheri Charboneau, National Accounts/
   University of Phoenix

"I made a comment many years ago about learning that Shaun grabbed onto and has since lived by. Learning makes us better leaders in our business, better friends, better for our families and better people. Take the time to learn from Shaun and you'll be enhanced in all these ways too."

—Dave Hatzung, President, Hatzung Insurance

"Shaun has taken his own personality and competitive advantage and laid it all out for you here to implement. It's not often you get a look behind the curtain at a system used by one of the best. You'd do well to pay attention and develop your own system using Shaun's words as a guide."

—Joe Hagan, *Freedom Through Systems*

# CONVERTIBLE REFERRALS

## SHAUN IRWIN

## How to Get
## More Referrals
## and More Clients

Convertible Referrals

Published by:
Convertible Referrals
www.convertiblereferrals.com

ISBN: 9780989152709

Cover design and photo: Stan Wai
Publishing and production management:
 Jim Bindas—Books & Projects
Printed by union labor

The Mustang logo and image are the exclusive property and trademark of Ford Motor Company. They did not approve or endorse this book or the content described in any way.

This book is dedicated to my brother Doug. He showed me that selling isn't selling at all; it was just fun getting to know people and helping them! He's always been my hero and always will be.

# FOREWORD

One of the most powerful images of "success" I have in my head is an older couple who are riding together in a red convertible—they are laughing as their hair dances in the wind.

Meeting Shaun Irwin brings that image to mind. It's rare in life that you meet people who are in synch with who they are in their work, their play, their faith, their giving, and their family. I've known Shaun more than a decade—it's been exciting and energizing to watch him basically be himself in all arenas of life.

So there is nothing contrived about this book. You will read that you need to be "ready to give" in order to receive. That's just Shaun being Shaun, because he lives those values each and every single day. This book will teach you how to get more by giving—but only if you are ready to see yourself in that red convertible . . .

I look forward to watching the referrals grow in your life, personally and professionally.

Paul Batz
Expert in Personal Leadership
Executive Coach, Professional Speaker
Author of *What Really Works—Blending the Seven Fs for the Life You Imagine: Faith, Family, Finances, Fitness, Friends, Fun and Future*

# PREFACE

The work we do in our organization is consultative in nature. To some, it's downright boring. They hear "insurance" and their eyes start to glaze over and they stammer a little while looking at their watch to see how long they must listen before excusing themselves to get coffee or, better yet, get to their root canal appointment.

My guess is that even though you like, or even love, what you do, your business is not very exciting to other people either.

Having attended thousands of meetings, lunches, happy hours, educational seminars, parties, and other assorted gatherings, I've discovered one topic everybody is excited to talk about: How Do You Grow Your Business?

At these gatherings it's common for us to spend significantly more time discussing business growth strategies rather than deductibles, risk transfer mechanisms, or business interruption worksheets.

People who run businesses are interested in how to make their businesses grow from the fledgling companies they started into powerhouses or, at a minimum, successful enough to comfortably support their families and their passion to be self-employed.

They *love* talking about themselves. Fortunately, I enjoy listening and I love to help. It gives me a huge charge to connect two people who can help each other be successful.

The excitement I've seen in their eyes and heard in their voices and the affirmation of their words helped me decide to write this book.

# My Story

When I moved from California to Minnesota in 1987 I knew exactly three people—my wife and her parents. I had no money, no job, no college degree, and an incredibly shaky marriage.

If you lived in Minneapolis in 1987 you would have seen an unemployed, fairly unkempt young pup arriving from San Diego. I would have been recognizable because I looked a little lost and was carrying the entirety of my worldly goods in the duffel bag hung over my shoulder.

People still constantly ask me why on God's green earth I moved from San Diego to Minnesota. Who does that? The simple answer is that I chased a girl. The more complicated and true answer is that I was 25 years old, with very few prospects, making a last-ditch attempt to save a marriage that ultimately was not going to be saved.

Not being aware of the job market in Minneapolis or, frankly, anywhere for that matter, I got to work with the classifieds, an actual newspaper with job ads in it. I didn't have a car or health insurance at the time. Let's face it—I was desperate.

I read an ad for the Anderson Agency that said they wanted a "licensed Minnesota Agent." Even though I didn't have an insurance license, I thought I could do the job and applied for the position. I managed to get a second interview in my brand new J.C. Penney suit but I was pretty sure that, even though they were being very nice to me, they weren't going to hire me.

I had one very good thing going for me: I could type like a madman possessed by demons and also had some limited computer experience. Long story short: I had taken typing in high school and did a short typing stint where I was paid to type by the piece. That took my fair typing skills and converted my fingers into gazelles. I liked the money that came with the limited time commitment to the piecework.

But even with that—and let's face it, they thought it was weird that a guy could type so fast—I still wasn't going to get hired.

It was two in the afternoon and my hand was on the door getting ready to leave when I noticed their IBM XT computer sitting on a desk, turned off. That's right, it wasn't even turned on. I know that may seem very odd in today's 24/7 age of smartphones and Twitter but there it was, the only computer in the office, turned off at two in the afternoon.

The owner of the agency was 55 years old and the man who was going to be my boss was 56. They weren't going to use the darn thing.

So in my brilliance (or desperation), I asked, "What are you doing with that computer?" They said, "We're going to use it to issue binders, invoices, policies," blah, blah, blah.

I said, "That's what I do" and I could see their entire demeanor change before my eyes. They had what they were looking for, sort of: an unlicensed, uneducated, uninsured, enthusiastic young man to answer the phones and open the mail . . . who knew how to turn on a computer. I was not a real sharp candidate for a meteoric rise to salesman, let alone a job with additional responsibility.

Oh yeah, I forgot to mention I also had a drinking problem. After having my near-subsistence entry-level job for a couple of years, my boss, an exceptionally good man, asked me about a trend he saw in my absenteeism. In general, Minnesota people are kind of nice to a fault, so I know how hard it must have been for him to talk about it. He wondered if I was aware that the days I missed work were always a Monday or Friday. He let me know he cared about me and could see my potential, but . . .

By this time I was separated from my wife and my only real connection to Minnesota was my job. I was more than a little lost.

Everyone was gone from the office that evening as I sat and thought about Lee and how much he must have cared about me to talk to me about his belief in me. I also thought about "Footprints in the Sand," a poem about the struggles in life.

Lee had watered a seed that had already been planted in my mind. I knew that for me, success meant happiness, a family, a career, and accomplishment.

I realized that in spite of all of the terrible hare-brained decisions I'd made in my life, someone was watching over me. It was time to find the road that would lead me to success.

I took out a sheet of paper and wrote "Success" across the top and then drew a line straight down the middle of the page. Then I wrote all the reasons I could be successful on the left-hand side and all the things that would hold me back on the right-hand side. I knew I was going to come head-to-head with the drinking. I resolved that was the day.

So I went out and bought a twelve pack of beer (Schlitz), a pint of vodka, and a quart of fruit juice. I drank it all that night and haven't touched a drink since.

**Today I own the company.**

"Successful people are always looking for opportunities to help others. Unsuccessful people are always asking, "What's in it for me?" —Brian Tracy

# I LEARNED

It was from that fairly awkward and humble beginning that I started my journey in learning about business. I've always been a curious sort anyway and I started asking questions of the insurance companies we worked with, our customers, our vendors—pretty much anyone who would talk to me.

I kept answering the phone and opening the mail and eventually got the computer to do something other than act as paperweight, all the while asking questions.

One thing my bosses did exceptionally well . . .

**they let me fail.**

If it didn't cost the agency money, they pretty much let me try it. They did want me to get a license since that's what they advertised in the first place, and they were willing to pay for it as long as I passed the test the first time. I was able to breeze through the licensing in pretty short order.

I quickly figured out that everybody seemed to love to talk about themselves and their businesses, especially about how they want to grow their businesses. I kept asking questions and kept learning.

Fast-forward a few years . . .

# TAKE TIME TO LEARN

Years ago I was introduced to Dave Hatzung of Hatzung Insurance, who said something that pierced my heart and soul in a way that few others have before or since. He said, "Most people finish school and believe that their education obligations have been filled, that they are done learning. I've come to the realization that we get to decide every day whether we want to be learners or not."

At that breakfast meeting on a snowy day in Edina, Minnesota, I committed to a lifetime of learning. It was a gift: Dave gave clarity to what I was already drawn to.

How about you?

**It's a given that you need to be good enough that people will be willing to refer someone to you or your business.**

## Do you know how many referrals you receive?

Especially in professional service firms, it's always fascinating to me that, with rare exceptions, when I ask people where they get most of their business they say "Referrals," but when questioned further, most people have no idea how often they receive referrals or have a system to track referrals.

Over the last decade my follow-up question has been, "How many referrals do you get a year?" After looking into the air for an answer they either make one up or give a nondescript answer like "A lot." If they know and track the referrals, I applaud them. If they admit to their own ignorance—and the good ones do—I ask, "How do you know it's a key source of business if you don't track the referrals and have no way to foster them?"

This begins the litany of descriptions about why their business is "different," how tracking "doesn't really translate," that the results from a referral might take longer to realize or cash in on than other businesses, why they can't really incentivize or systematize referrals, etc.

To this I would argue that they are missing the greatest advantage they can ever give their businesses. Professional service firms, in particular, grow dramatically from having customer referral systems in place; most of us are just too busy running around shaking hands and slapping people on the back like politicians to stop long enough to quantify the volume and organize the best methodology to grow our businesses through referrals, even though that growth can be exponential.

Good news for you today, ladies and gentlemen, because I've done it and will share what I've learned with you.

**Getting referrals is simple, but**
***converting referrals* into clients is what matters!**

Everybody says they grow and succeed with referrals. You're going to be able to grow and prove it to yourself, your employees, and your banker, and you'll gain more freedom from worry while you're doing it.

It is possible to carve out a successful career without a definitive process or system for referrals. It's called the willy-nilly, hope-and-chance method. I'm not too keen on that.

The number of wasted referrals each and every year is staggering. It's estimated that 79% of referrals are never even contacted! Of the referrals that are contacted (remember, that's only 21%), nearly 91% are only contacted once and then forgotten. What we'll illustrate in this book is how to dramatically and systematically increase the number of referrals you receive and, better yet, how to convert those referrals into long-term lucrative relationships with people who will, in turn, refer you more . . . *Convertible Referrals*.

# Referrals are a two-way street

My feelings run deep and strong when it comes to joining groups but if you are singularly focused on yourself and *your* success, put this book down now; stop wasting your time reading it. You may be wildly successful but it won't be because of referrals because . . .

## *Referrals are born from giving.*

If you are solely a taker you will never be the beneficiary of the greater good of giving. The law of reciprocity is constantly at work in the universe and referrals are an outstanding example of its balance.

I had an indelible mark left on me regarding this when I was a young professional (I'm using the term "professional" loosely referring to my younger years). Early in my career we didn't have anyone in our group tracking referrals but I tracked mine on a weekly basis. I tracked where all of my business came from, but the referrals I gave and kept I really just tracked through a running list. I didn't tally them until the end of the year, but when I did I learned I had given 51 referrals and, lo and behold, I received 51 referrals. I would have to have been a fool not to see the Law of Reciprocity at work. That life lesson has stuck like glue.

Now when I want to find a way to grow a relationship I try to find ways to help the other people grow in their success. Take that a step further, if you dare, and make it a goal not to *get* referrals but to *give* referrals. I know it sounds revolutionary but I guarantee you that if you think of others they'll be thinking of you. If you think about only yourself it will be a party that you attend alone before too long.

Even people who know you and like you are not likely to open their most valuable and intimate business relationships to you unless they see the benefit to them or to their friends, family, and/or customers.

# Join a group. Better yet, join multiple groups

Joining a formal networking group that is focused on exchanging business, that will help you tighten your unique selling proposition and expand your circle of influence and trust, is a vital component of a referral system, for yourself and your entire sales team. The group(s) you join should have the following components:

- Gratitude
- Weekly meetings
- Spotlight on a business each week
- Way to track referrals
- At least 10 members, preferably fewer than 20
- Breakfast or lunch meetings lasting no more than 1–1.5 hours (I prefer breakfast meetings.)
- Decent private settings
- Regular attendance (better at breakfast meetings)
- Rotating leadership
- Education-Business-Wellness-Financial—diverse professions within the group

The importance of most of these is self-evident but I'll touch on a few for reinforcement.

Gratitude is the way for the referral merry-go-round to continue spinning. Without it you will be building your business some other way because referrals will dry up. The consistent message of gratitude and giving of your time, energy, and talents is the surest way to get more referrals. Countless times I've received an additional referral simply by calling and updating a person about the referral he or she gave me, that I'd reached out to the referral even if I didn't end up doing business with them.

Many people fear sharing with the referring party when a referral doesn't quite fit their business or just isn't something that they do. You can use this opportunity to sincerely and expansively thank a person and give them a clearer picture of who the best fit is for your company.

Networking groups are built on trust and you need to spend time with each other to build trust in one another. Monthly meetings simply don't allow enough chances for people to grow closer to one another and build a trust bank. If you're gone one month and I happen to be gone the next, three months pass between seeing one another. That's not a networking relationship; that's an acquaintance that you run into every now and again. It's pretty easy to understand how it can happen: you're gone one month for a very legitimate reason—vacation, illness, client presentation, etc.—and your networking cohort is gone the next month, voilà! You haven't seen each other in three months.

Weekly meetings also give you, as a member of the group, the practice required to hone your "Unique Selling Proposition," to explain why someone should do business with you above any and all other choices.

The right group should be a very safe environment with people you know to hone your message.

Most business networking groups give each member just a minute or two to give their very concise elevator speech or share a referral or an update on a referral given to them. However, the Spotlight Person typically gets 10 to 15 minutes to expand on their business model, share a particularly illustrative success story or, if they choose, to ask for help with a business problem. I wouldn't take this time to discuss a business problem but I've seen it done. I've also seen many people waste this time by not being prepared. This is a bad, bad, bad idea.

It's also a terrible idea to think that people "already know" what you do and who your ideal customer is. Try to remember right now where someone in your church, Rotary club, kid's sports programs, or even a casual friend works, how you could help them in their job, and who their ideal customer is. You'll find that it's far more difficult than you think.

Guess what? People won't remember how to help *you* unless you use this time effectively to clearly articulate and paint a picture for them. Use your spotlight time to ask for help and lay out a strategic direction for your business, or simply expand on why you are the right choice for them to refer their family, friends, and business contacts. Building the confidence within your group is very important when you only get to be in the spotlight once every few months.

This is also an ideal time to reach someone in your group you think could give you more referrals but you've been unable to connect with to foster a deeper connection. Getting in touch with them before or after your spotlight time reinforces your credibility and will get them thinking about you specifically. They'll listen more closely to your presentation.

Take the opportunity to meet one person each week one on one as well. If you have a good number of people in your group (10 to 15) you should be able to meet with each person individually once a quarter or so. Those one-on-one meetings allow you to dig deeper to learn about the other person's business and how you can help them succeed. Whether you are able to or not, they will appreciate you spending the time with them to get to know them better and trying to facilitate their success.

Join groups to share your time, treasure, and talents with other people who share your giving heart. Learning with other people about interesting things will help lift a group because as everyone becomes more inquisitive you'll be asking each other more questions about ways you can help one another.

I wasn't that interested in learning things that colleges thought were interesting; I was, and continue to be, interested in learning about people, persuasion, and business.

## Adding and subtracting members

People will drop out of your networking group for several reasons. The group may not fit in their current lifestyle or they just don't perceive a value. If and when they leave your group, evaluate for yourself whether this is a relationship you want to continue to cultivate. You should have a very good idea by then whether they are givers or takers.

One-on-one meetings can also facilitate recruiting for your networking group if you brainstorm together about what kind of other professionals would be a good fit for your group. It's very important that you continue to recruit high-quality members for your group.

Keep momentum in the group by adding more members. The group should provide lots of value for someone coming into it. Don't add someone just for the sake of adding them; be diligent about adding quality people, though when you personally bring them into the group, you will almost always benefit more than the other members of the group. Everyone else will be thrilled to have another productive member in the group, someone who will offer referrals.

Make it a point to visit with new members you don't know within the first month they join your group. Just like a new customer, they are evaluating whether they made a good decision to join your group. By spending time with them they'll be impressed with your group, appreciative of your interest, and think of you when the time comes for them to help someone.

I didn't have the good sense to do it years ago but I would now include them in our company newsletter, marketing, and events. Who better to market to and for you than someone you see every week? There will be more about newsletters and events later in this book.

# Be prepared

The more people you're meeting with, the more structure you should have for the agenda, but for any and all formats you should be ready for success. Prepare for a business meeting just like you would prepare for a date.

At breakfast meetings, is there any reason you shouldn't be there 15 minutes early to review your notes? Breakfast or coffee is often a time to meet, greet, have a group gathering, or an educational seminar.

Coffee/breakfast is an outstanding way to start a business Circle of Influence dialogue or customer relationship. A Circle of Influence person is someone you've noticed and identified as a thought leader, a mover and shaker in their area of expertise or customer relationships, or a magnet of influence. I've met some amazing technicians but they aren't always very influential.

Lunch-and-learns are growing in popularity but are usually done at a (preferably a customer's) place of business.

By the way, if you're meeting at a coffee shop nobody feels like they are beholden to a structured sit-down-who's-going-to-pay-what-kind-of-restaurant-is-it mental hopscotch.

When you're meeting somebody you can help, by all means plan out intervals for communication that will help the relationship grow. Have a series of communications already in the queue. When you can make a direct connection to a business connection or customer, it's fairly easy to grow the relationship.

The most common gaping hole, sometimes the size of the Grand Canyon, is when there is no direct decision-maker or current opportunity that you are aware of. By asking yourself a quick series of questions coming out of the meeting, you'll be able to assess and execute on the valuable time you spent meeting with the potential partner/Circle of Influence/mentor.

# TWO EARS

There's an old expression in sales that God gave us two ears and only one mouth because we should listen twice as much as we speak. A variation of that can be cited for the great referral sources in your group. They need to be able to listen twice, once to you as you describe your ideal referral and once to their customer, friend, or business relationship so they can describe a need you can fill. Without both of those critical skills they'll never be an exceptional referral source.

# WISE ADVICE

During one meeting, a wise man in our group said that his Rolodex (a definite sign of another age and time) "doesn't stop on 'anybody.'" What he meant is when you are looking for referrals, it's less likely you'll get them if you say, "I'm a real estate agent looking for anybody who wants to buy or sell a house."

A minor refinement could do wonders—"I'm a residential real estate agent and just listed a house in Edina. Do you know anyone looking for a home there?" or "I'm looking for friends or coworkers you know who live in the Sunnyside neighborhood of the city. I have a client who is looking for a house there . . ." Or, "Couples tend to buy when they're in transition—just married, or whose kids will start school within two years, or recent 'empty-nesters.' If you know anybody on that list, it would be great to hear about them."

Try to be concise, but be specific when recruiting referrals.

# SPOTLIGHT ON ELLEN

Ellen McDonough took the networking strategy to a level of specificity that consistently generated referrals for her. A business travel specialist, Ellen came to each meeting armed with the names of five companies, including each company's business travel manager and CEO, that she wanted to do business with.

Ellen prepared us to help her succeed and, more often than not, we did. She also didn't quit doing it just because it didn't work one week. She knew if she did her homework it would click with someone that, yes indeed, they did know Sally at Technichrome or Bill at Goodlick's.

If you are prepared on a consistent basis, other people in the group will be too, especially as it relates to your relationship with them.

# Invite the best

**"You are the average of the five people you spend the most time with."**
—Jim Rohn, entrepreneur and author

The saying goes that you should hang around with people you want to be most like. That's the fundamental reason parents get nervous if their little angels start hanging around with a "bad crowd." We know that people we choose to spend a great deal of time with will impact our lives positively and negatively. What stops many people from seeking out the best is their mistaken assumption that the "best" people won't take the time to help them succeed. While it's true that there are successful people who are myopically obsessed with only their own well-being, I think it's far rarer than most young or medium upstarts think. Don't plan to waste their time but if you're prepared to listen well, learn, and execute on advice, I believe you'll find more than enough mentors to help you gain purchase in your given field and beyond.

The Internet has forever changed the amount of access we all have to information. There is absolutely no barrier to the greatest business minds of all time in books, audios, blogs, or white papers. The access to material in any given pursuit is there for a fraction of its real value if only you pursue it. Ask people in your industry who they think are the smartest, most successful, caring people they know and they'll be happy to tell you. Then call those people, stop by, or send them a note. Find out their interests and seek them out. Ask them if they'll mentor you. Some may flatly refuse, others might put conditions on it, and still others may defer, but you'll collect great minds with solid advice.

Be prepared to be challenged. All progress starts with the truth. Do you have a plan for success that you can share with these great minds? What are the specific questions you want to ask each one in your interview process? Do you currently have a job or are you working on a career? Think about what you want your career to look like in one, three, or five years.

Most important: Do you intend to listen and execute or are you solely soliciting the magic bullet?

Be ready to be held accountable. Busy, successful people want to help and inspire others; they don't want to waste time repeatedly going over the same things. Listen well, take notes, be prepared to make commitments, and then execute. If it doesn't work you'll have far more to discuss than if you didn't get to it at all or went at it half-baked.

# RELATIONSHIPS

Don Phin, CEO of HR That Works and author of *Victims, Villains and Heroes: Managing Emotions in the Workplace*: http://www.donphin.com/victimsvillains.asp, captures relationships quite well when he says: "There is no such thing as a 50/50 relationship. Our energy is usually weaker or stronger. Sometimes a person might give 80 and at other times the other person gives 20, but anytime a relationship is too one-sided it erodes over time. Fact is, all relationships need space to survive. Good relationships that are long-term positive operate in the corridor of 40/20/40. What we call 'Playing 40/40.' The room in the middle is for the dance. For the co-creation. Only at 40/40 can we both be heroes in a relationship!" He's quick to point out that this is true of all relationships, not just business relationships.

## Does networking work?

A few years after I got my insurance license one of my very first coworkers and I got a huge laugh when a salesman who had lived in Minnesota his entire life told her that the only reason I had the most sales in the company was because of all the people I knew. Huh?

Now, then, and frankly anytime, the only barrier to meeting the people you want to meet and do business with is your process for getting introduced to them.

# Associations

Business associations, whether for-profit or nonprofit, are designed to make money for the association's leadership, specifically the Executive Director. This is not to contend that they don't bring value to members. In fact, they have to bring value to their members or members will no longer be willing to pay dues. It may sound like I have a problem with it but I don't; it's simply a premise you must recognize if you want to grow your business through association-referral marketing.

The very best association leaders are like other business leaders—they have a passion for their members and the customers their members serve. By understanding the success of the organization (how well it works) and how the leaders make it work, you'll be better able to position yourself as an expert to the membership and help the association make more money and grow. When you choose to join an association, take note of how the committees are organized and where you can provide value. There is nothing more fun than having someone call and say, "Andy told me to call you, that you can help us ..."

A suggestion I often hear is to join the membership committee. In my particular field, it works far better to be part of an education committee so I can be recognized as a subject expert and be able to use it in the future for more targeted marketing for our firm when building relationships.

Referrals from respected, trusted advisors are gold. The normal reticence of a potential client is eased when someone they truly respect refers them to you. Association memberships, often correctly, give the impression that your expertise makes you the better professional to hire. They certainly give you access to the common vernacular, challenges, regulations, triumphs, and industry conversations going on in that field . . . if you're willing to listen and learn.

Make sure you get a list of all new association members each month. Call them and ask them why they joined and what they are hoping to get out of their membership (they'll be shocked you did). If it aligns with your vision, by all means make an appointment to learn more about them and help them to understand how the association is organized. Share what you've learned to help them be successful; you'll never regret it.

Another fruitful ground is the social aspect the meeting or educational event offers, but it's interesting to observe the people who come for a morning session and don't take advantage of the time to socialize. They bury their heads in their Crackberries or iPhones while they could be building relationships. Others simply take off physically when dismissed but have mentally checked out ten to twenty minutes earlier.

**We're all busy!** Make the time you spend at association functions count:

- Let a prospect-member know you'll be there. See if you can spend time with him/her.
- Try to set it up so one of your customers in the association invites a prospect to sit with you and your customer at the event.
- Be early and introduce yourself to each person who comes. Yes, I know: "It's so hard." "I don't want to bother anyone." "It feels weird"— blah, blah, blah.
- Find out something about the speaker to share with the folks at your table or around you. You'll be very surprised that most people don't do a simple search to find out any information about the speaker. I always take the time to thank the speaker for sharing his or her time with us. If he or she is someone I want to meet later, they almost always remember me when I call and want to get together.
- Make the lunch, breakfast, or social event a priority but don't eat too much, drink too much, or hang with one person too much.
- Ask first: find out what people do and what drives them. Ask why they came to the event and what they hope to get out of it. It will give you something to follow up on after the event.
- Leave enough time to make notes in your Customer Relationship Manager (your database can be index cards if they work for you, but most people have computerized notes nowadays with actions and steps to reconnect). It's insane how many leads and referrals get kicked into the sewer because people don't follow-up.

- Execute a specific follow-up plan for each contact you made or wanted to make. For example, if you intended to see someone at the event but you didn't, send a note saying just that and invite them to meet.

When you get an opportunity to speak at an association event on a panel or as a featured speaker, invite the specific people you want to see you to the event. It's best to use multiple media to do this but even using one, such as a postcard or personal email (not a group email) to promote your involvement will boost the likelihood of attendance and referrals.

When people thank you for speaking, ask about them. You're flying high after a good speaking event and you're the "expert"; find out what they are expert at and follow up. They'll be flattered and definitely make the time for you.

Have someone record your presentation, then listen to it and distribute it to those people you most want to connect with that you think will be interested in your talk.

# BREAKING BREAD TOGETHER

Everybody needs to eat. Breaking bread together has had significant cultural implications for thousands of years. The very act of eating together and filling our bodies with nourishment brings us closer. Study after study indicates families grow closer and their ties stronger when they eat together. It's important, whether you realize it or not.

I highly recommend Keith Ferrazzi's book, *Never Eat Alone: And Other Secrets to Success, One Relationship at a Time*: http://keithferrazzi.com/products/never-eat-alone. Breaking bread (or doughnuts) with people is life changing, especially in today's distracted, electronic environment. When you can, make it part of your plan to select specific people to eat breakfast, lunch, and dinner with. If it helps, you can even segment it this way: breakfast/coffee to meet, lunch to grow, and dinner to thank. Let's break it down a little more:

## Breakfast

Is this somebody I'd want to refer a customer to or I think can/would refer customers to me? Is this somebody who works for or owns (preferably) a company I would like to do business with? Is this someone I would like on my board of directors?

## Lunch

That gets us to lunch. You can start with lunch if you'd like but I would only do that if coffee/breakfast scheduling doesn't work. Lunch is to woo and introduce others in person. You host lunch to walk up the ladder of importance with people and be willing to share your key relationships with them. Lunch should be where the prospect/future customer/relationship builder will be happy and feel comfortable.

A tangent here on lunch before golf. A quick lunch with minimal business conversation before golf is best. Offer your prospect/customer a chance to invite someone along, even though most times they won't. Try to schedule golf when they don't have to race off afterward, but if they don't force the business discussion at the end, save it. The two-step will do you far more than the rush.

## Dinner

Invite every key referral relationship (with their spouse and/or partner) to dinner at the most expensive restaurant you can afford. Dinner is a commitment on your part and theirs that you are in a relationship. The conversation will allow you to get to know each other in a way you probably aren't quite as familiar with and will enable you to also get an endorsement from the one whose opinion they value very greatly.

Spend time asking at least three questions of the spouse or partner to learn more about them and their interests. Let them dominate the conversation if they want, and it shouldn't have to be said but I'll say it anyway: Don't drink too much. If they are drinkers don't get in the way of their drinking but don't have more than one or two cocktails yourself. Many a budding deal has gone south over the slip of the tongue after alcohol.

The dinner environment also allows you to explore more points of connectivity that will foster growth in the relationship. You can invite the person and maybe even his or her spouse to interact at a more frequent or deeper level.

Dr. Paul Voss, Ethikos, www.ethikos.com's founder and president, supports the theory that something changes in the brain when we "break bread together." Research shows a deeper connection when sharing a meal than just having a discussion. Food plays an integral role in breaking barriers to communication and accelerates our connections.

I must admit that it all sounds good on paper but it's not something that I'm able to execute effectively. I am open to sharing meals when schedules align but I'm not caught up on the specifics of which meal fits for each stage. I understand it but with my busy family life it's more important to me to align my schedule with my family than work opportunities.

# Say no
## when you have to

I'm frequently astonished when I hear a professional say they don't want to do business with their friends or family. They want to "separate" their personal and professional lives. It's the dumbest thing I've ever heard. Think about it: What you're saying is "I'm too nervous that I won't do a stellar job for my family" or you're saying you care so little about them that you would rather they deal with strangers.

Say no to friends and relatives if it's not what you do and you don't know where to align them with the right people, but don't say no out of fear. The very best way to help your family and friends is to listen and help them when you can. You don't have to force the issue of business at all. Help them get jobs, be interested in what their kids are doing, listen to things that are important to them. In other words, treat them as well as you would strangers and the business relationship will happen when they are ready to ask you to help.

The very best and most talented people I've ever met say no all the time. I recently read a blog by Darren Hardy, publisher of *Success* magazine, that really struck home. He said people have genuine difficulty saying no to people and want to say yes. The reality is that every time you say yes to something you are saying no to something else because you just filled your time with whatever you said yes to.

Happily standing next to the 2005 National Marketer of the Year prize!

Handing over the winner's check to our Tapemark Charity Pro Am professional winner.

Celebrating the Marketer of the Year award with my friends.

Gratefully giving to the Emergency Food Shelf Network.

Yes, this is the car we gave away.

Doing fun and interesting things together brings your team closer.

Everyone wins with referrals.

MAY
2012
VOLUME 6,
ISSUE 5

NEWS AND INFORMATION FROM THE ANDERSON-BRAINERD PROTECTION TEAM

# In the Know

## Do You Need ID Theft Insurance?

Alarming new statistics show that one in every 20 Americans has now been a victim of identity theft and the crime is climbing by about 13 percent a year. Identity theft involves somebody pretending to be you. It leads to a wide range of crimes, from people using your credit card information to make purchases to those who use your name to get loans, get healthcare and even get a job.

Crooks get their information from a variety of sources including stolen cards and records or by piecing together information that's publicly available on the Internet. Personal details, like credit card and Social Security numbers are traded in the crime underworld for about a dollar each. Often, victims don't find out about the crime until they get a huge credit card bill or a finance company chases them for an unpaid debt.

There are lots of things you can do to reduce the risk of becoming a victim. You'll find plenty of guidance on a special website set up by the Federal Trade Commission (FTC) at http://tinyurl.com/ftc-id-theft-guide. But even the most stringent precautions can't totally protect you. So, can and should you insure against the risk? It depends.

First, it's important to know that with credit card fraud - the most common type of ID theft - the limit of your liability is usually $50. The card companies have to eat the rest. Banks also have to carry the burden of debit card and check fraud. Likewise, if someone steals your ID to claim a tax refund, the IRS will normally still honor your entitlement.

Other instances may result in a substantial loss for which you may need insurance - loss of earnings for example. You may find you already have some protection in your homeowner's insurance policy, so check that first. Call us today and we'd be happy to do a review for you. Additional, separate coverage may be available but as with most types of insurance, this will have a deductible and a limit on the maximum payout. Some policies will provide a counselor to provide advice on clearing your name and unraveling the mess that often follows in the wake of identity theft, which could be a real plus.

Ultimately, the most important thing you can do to protect yourself is to avoid giving away personal information and to regularly scrutinize bank and credit card statements. The sooner you take action, the less impact the crime will have.

It can happen to anyone, don't let it happen to you!

**Thank You!**

**Thank You!**

**Thank You!**

*Tony Tellijohn*

Tony is the winner of this month's Referral Program drawing!

He will receive a $25 Target Gift Card - just for sending someone our way!

Customer education, acknowledgement, and gratitude go a long way.

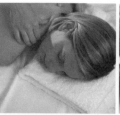

# Protecting your business and home isn't a luxury...

## yet.

For over 80 years, Anderson Agency has been providing rock solid protection for businesses and homes across Minnesota. It may not be glamorous, but it's what we do best.

In 2008, we're looking to inject a little luxury into the lives of those who have helped our business grow – including Tapemark Charity Pro-Am golfers and supporters. So, we're giving away a 2008 Ford Mustang GT Convertible, along with 19 other prizes, all to lucky winners who send people our way this year. It's our way of adding a little bit of pleasure and excitement to the lives of the people who are helping us succeed.

Check out some of the other great prizes we're giving away in 2008:

- Weekend Getaways
- Flowers for a year
- Day at the spa
- Decadent Chocolate Basket
- Much, much more!

**Call Shaun Irwin at 612-236-1784 today to learn more and get in on the excitement!**

## Anderson Agency

*Presenting Sponsor of the 37th annual Tapemark Charity Pro-Am*

Phone: 612-236-1784      Toll Free: 866-810-3030      Web: www.andersonagencyins.com

Communicate your referral process as many ways as you can.

# Win a BIG SCREEN TV compliments of the Anderson-Brainerd Protection Team!

### *To qualify, just send us a referral!*
### *One lucky person will win a BIG SCREEN TV!*

*"Thank you for providing us with many years of great customer service. You have always had our best interests at heart when it comes to our insurance needs and have never hesitated to meet our expectations. You are truly customer-focused and always go out of your way to ensure that we are receiving the best insurance coverage that will meet and fulfill our needs!"*
-Tim & Monica Andrew, 2010 Referral Program Winners

## WIN BIG IN 2011!

We're dedicated to taking special care of you and all of our clients. We value the loyalty of our clients and the quality referrals they send our way. As a "thank you" for helping us succeed, we're going to make you a winner!

We're giving you the opportunity to **WIN BIG** in 2011! All you have to do is refer us to your family, friends and co-workers. We'll provide *them* with competitive rates, reliable protection and exceptional customer service. Even better, we'll make you a winner every time, and give you a chance to win one of our wonderful monthly and yearly grand prizes!

**Why wait?! YOU are in control of how many chances you have to WIN BIG! Get started TODAY by calling us toll-free at 1-866-710-3030, or use the back of this sheet!**

| **CHANCE 1** | Every time you send a referral our way, you'll win:<br>• $5 gas card<br>• $15 to the charity of your choice |
| --- | --- |
| **CHANCE 2** | The first week of each month, we'll randomly draw from all of last month's Chance 1 qualifiers.<br>• The winner will receive a $25 Target Gift Card |
| **CHANCE 3** | In January 2012, we'll conduct a random drawing from all qualified chances from 2011:<br>• The GRAND PRIZE winner will receive a BIG SCREEN TV!<br>• The Charity Grand Prize winner will have $500 donated to the charity of their choice. |

Please see reverse side for Referral Program rules.

Referral incentives can be small and large.

Giving back because it's the right thing to do.

# Remember them . . .
## but don't fake it

If your memory isn't good enough to remember other people's interests, then develop a system for yourself that allows you to refresh your memory before you speak or meet with them. A word of caution here: If you don't really care about their family or their interests, it will be revealed in your speech and attention. In other words, don't be tempted to fake it; it won't work. That's in part why building relationships with people who at least have connections in meaningful areas of your life makes sense. It helps if you really do care that their kids have a band because you are into music.

If you are particularly challenged about either note taking or memory, especially people's names, there are executive memory coaches who can help you with strategies to improve in this area.

Names, names, names! People will say "I'm really good with faces; I just can't remember names." You won't help yourself at all if you remember someone's face and then get the question-mark bubble over your head regarding their name. Learn to remember names better! Short of that, practice a confident smile in the mirror, stride up, and say your name. If they remember you they'll say "I know," and will give their name. You'll be back in action.

**Our favorite sound is the sound of our own name.**

That is "Names 1.5." "Names 2.0 or 3.0" is remembering the name of their spouse or, better yet, their children. A spouse's name can change; children's names rarely do. My wife and I were in a grocery store a few years back and ran into a customer we both knew. My wife admits she is not good at remembering names. I remembered the woman's name, which was no big deal, but I also remembered her daughter's name and said hello to her. The change in the woman's facial expression clearly showed that she was happy that I not only acknowledged her daughter but remembered her name. Names matter because they are such a huge part of our identity. If you're bad at it, taking the time to get better at it will be time well spent. Taking the time to be great at it, if you can, will make you golden. You'll make people feel better about themselves because they were memorable. You'll have instant rapport and credibility and make more money because of it.

# PHILANTHROPY

Service on nonprofit boards or religious organizations should be joined solely for what you can give. Not everyone looks at it this way, especially in a service organization, but that's my take on it. Because of the law of reciprocity and people inherently wanting to be in relationships with people like themselves, business naturally flows from these groups the more you give, but getting business shouldn't be your intention.

I've done a series of presentations for businesses on how to bring philanthropy into their workplaces so they can be better stewards in the cities where their businesses are located. Becoming a multiplier through example and showing immense gratitude for the city supporting their businesses is always rewarding. I know that giving has done far more for me than I've ever been able to give.

I'm a member of the City of Lakes Rotary in Minneapolis. At the time I joined our children were 6 and 4. They were not quite into sports yet but were starting to be involved in the various kid activities that take up multiple nights and weekends. I wanted to give back to our community with like-minded people but didn't necessarily have time to organize the events or activities. Rotary was a perfect outlet to get plugged into. I was able to help on projects that were already set up by various people in our club.

I had zero business expectations from the group

but where trust grows, relationships follow. Working, singing (yes, we sing at our Rotary), and spending time together hand in hand, leads to people getting to know you better and wanting to help you. Without any expectations for business growth from Rotary, it's led to multiple business relationships and, yes, a considerable amount of money for our firm.

Since joining Rotary I've heard it said by a couple of different members this way: "If you join Rotary for business you'll be disappointed; if you join to give, your business will be better for it." I agree with that sentiment wholeheartedly.

## What can happen

Anecdotes about why referrals are critical are legendary: "I met a guy in a bar who referred me to the president of a *huge* corporation that became our customer on a million-dollar deal." Or "I play basketball with a woman who introduced me to her boss, the CEO of a national company and they became our customer," etc., etc., etc.

I have my own, which I'll share because stories are fun and it also illustrates why it's critical to develop a system to get more home runs or "Rembrandt referrals."

I was in a networking group that met on a weekly basis when I was a "still-wet behind-the-ears" salesman. It was a good, solid bunch of young professionals with a few seasoned veterans to round out the group. I was quite curious about one of the "old guys" because he was most accurately described as a "curmudgeon." My personality is exceedingly upbeat, his . . . not so much. But he must have been a good tactician because he worked on great projects and kept himself consistently busy in the marketing and advertising world. He would immerse himself in his projects and seemed to rarely come up for air. At that point in my work life, I still thought of marketing and advertising as the "big idea," Flo from Progressive, or the Geico Gecko. I didn't yet realize that marketing is 5% the "big idea" or the Aflac duck, and 95% organization and execution.

The curmudgeon didn't give a lot of referrals so I was a little shocked one day when he told me to call one of his friends who was working on a new project. Remember, I was very inexperienced, and I'm guessing my unbounded enthusiasm for the world in front of me was not in exact alignment with this grizzled savvy marketing executive. I figured if he told me to call the guy it must be really important, so I did.

Charlie was glad I called and yes, indeed, it would be good to meet me but of course he was very busy. Understanding the pressing time issues of a highly compensated executive (I really didn't understand at all—I could barely find my heinie with two hands), I suggested that we have lunch, figuring everyone has to eat and I could get his attention for at least an hour.

Not having any idea at all where to go for a productive and impressive business lunch, I asked him where he would like to go. Charlie suggested a place called Azur, which sounded really cool to me. I made reservations, wore my freshly dry-cleaned J.C. Penney suit (yep, the same one I wore to my interview), and showed up fifteen minutes early, excited to have a real business lunch and, hopefully, get some real business.

My anxiety level heightened as I read the menu (this was pre-Internet, so there was no checking out the menu ahead of time). I was doing the math in my head and calculating that lunch—*lunch,* mind you—might cost me close to $100. I love food but I didn't even know there were restaurants in Minneapolis, or anywhere in the Midwest, where two people could spend $100 on lunch.

I didn't have $100 on me and I wasn't sure my credit card limit would allow me to charge another $100. Uh oh! I went from very excited to anxiously trying to figure out what I should do if they rejected my credit card after lunch.

Charlie showed up and was a great guy about fifteen or twenty years older than I (though I had aged some in the previous 15 minutes). He seemed to like me and I put my anxiety on the back shelf as I heard about his grand plans for the next opportunity that was taking shape in his business. He was in real estate and was working on a commercial redevelopment project that was coming together . . . if he could get a couple more financing pieces in place.

I was really having a wonderful time in my big-boy suit at the fancy restaurant talking about real business deals—it was pretty heady stuff. I got the least expensive thing on the menu and, fortunately, Charlie decided to eat light as well. The bill came to $53 and I held my breath as I handed over my often-maxed-out credit card. Back came the lovely server, smiling, for my signature. My relief at being able to pay the bill lifted my spirits even more.

Of course, I had no idea of all the things that could derail a commercial redevelopment project or that "waiting to finalize a couple of key financing pieces" meant he didn't have the money yet to do the project. I simply forged ahead with certainty that Charlie was a brilliant real estate mogul that was just days away from hiring me to be his insurance agent for the project, and certain that when he saw how sharp and energetic I was he would need me for all his future projects.

Fortunately, for everyone involved, Charlie and his associates did pull off the project. I did have the time, energy, and curiosity to figure it out quite well and impressed Charlie and his associates. The $53 lunch turned into $7,954 in revenue for me that year and $351,625 (yes, I keep close track) since then. People who pay attention and do good work will be rewarded with referrals but why not get more, help more people with your special skills, and bring a bigger bag of deposits to your bank?

# Work on your business —
# Not in it!

Let's face it: At some level most of us are technicians of some sort. Oh please, I can hear you now: "No I'm not. I'm an artist (or an engineer, designer, lawyer, or other 'professional.'" What I mean by "technician" is that we're drawn to the work we do, but not necessarily to the type of work we need to do to attract more work. It's easy to put our nose down and focus on getting the work we have in front of us done, instead of allocating time and energy to generate future work.

Some people find any excuse in the world to not engage in the business of gaining new customers. People do it in fits and spurts or try to delegate it to the "marketing" department. Author Dan S. Kennedy's "No B.S. Marketing" maxim of not ending any business day without at least one activity that will lead to a new client is an excellent strategy for each of us to practice. Knowing your math makes it that much more meaningful to pursue.

If I asked you right now to tell me the average value of each of your customer relationships, how long would it take you to come up with an answer? What if I asked you the average value for customer relationships you've added in the last three years?

Could you find the answers in less than ten minutes for either one of those questions? I hope so because it's the building block not only for a referral process but also for any marketing program you're going to pursue.

Let's stick with "referral math" for a minute. Is your conversion ratio from a referral going to be higher than from other prospect sources? In my experience, the answer is a resounding yes.

The answer often gets somewhat murky when I ask a business owner or salesperson what their conversion ratios are for referrals and other sources of leads. It's not critical for this discussion to know the conversion percentages for all lead sources if you can buy into the premise that it will be higher, or better than satisfactory, with referrals, but you should do your math on all of your lead sources.

What are you willing to spend to attract referrals? Start with a quick look at where your new customer relationships have come from in the last two years. Add up the number of referrals you converted into customers, their average value, and the total. Depending on your business, there will be multiple transactions over the lifetime of a client; add/multiply the lifetime value of a client.

For our business, which is rich in aggregated industry statistics, a conservative lifetime value is 7.5 times the one-year revenue of the first transaction. You should be able to find credible statistics for your industry through industry associations or the experience of your own organization. Our average is actually over 20% better than the industry average but I use the more conservative measure for calculating return on investment (ROI). I also don't include the referral multiplier value that comes with each referral conversion.

Our statistics show that a person who came to us through a referral introduction is five times as likely to refer someone else, compared to someone who came from another lead source. That starts to be really fancy math, which isn't necessary to make the point that a commitment to a referral process needs to become part of your corporate culture.

Referrals have meant millions in revenue for our relatively small organization and we have the math and new customers to prove it. A big reason our retention and lifetime value is higher than our industry's average is because of the psychological power of referrals and our public referral process.

Do you suppose it's easier or harder to break a relationship after you've referred your friend, relative, or coworker to that company? Of course it's much harder to quit on that relationship after you validated it by referring someone to their company. Now, does it make it even harder to leave the relationship when you are publicly acknowledged for the referral and receive thanks in multiple steps and media forms?

You walk a loyalty ladder from transaction to raving fan in emotional sequences that you're not even aware are happening. It happens in our lives in so many settings that we don't even think about it, but they are deeply affecting our emotional/reptilian brains.

Without an organizational commitment to a referral process, it is scattershot at best and territorial at worst.

Even people who don't refer others will be more likely to stay longer because you publicly acknowledge those who refer. They see people continue to refer you, people like them, and it validates their staying with you.

Along with public acknowledgment you should have a referral reward process that is both an attraction and retention tool. Measure the results based on increased new relationships and I am extremely confident you will find your math to be eye-poppingly favorable. Here's an example of our math for a one-year period.

| Referral Reward | Annual Cost | Revenue |
|---|---|---|
| Mailers | $1,211 | |
| Prizes | $2,747 | |
| Donations | $1,765 | |
| Total Cost | $5,723 | |
| First Year | | $89,792 |

Lifetime Value  $673,440.

| First Year Return on Investment | 15.68 to 1 |
|---|---|
| Lifetime Return on Investment | 117.67 to 1 |

# Get your whole team on board

What definitely needs enhancing in our program is the number of times we mention our referral program and process to our customers and our team. I haven't come across an organization yet that communicates it too much. It's difficult to get sales and service team members to mention it enough because it feels to them as though they are talking about it all the time, even though they are not, because they have so many instances where they are having multiple conversations with the same customers.

It's an odd phenomenon that you can get relatively low-paid employees to ask, "Do you want fries with that?" or "Do you want a muffin with your coffee?" but a higher-paid employee cannot execute a straightforward referral.

Ask questions of your employees. Ask with a carrot, a hammer, provide consistent coaching, follow up, do your best cajoling, follow up again, add incentives.

It is my belief that it's an unwillingness or inability on the part of the management team to consistently train, monitor, retrain, adjust, and communicate the program to their organization. The old "what gets measured gets done" adage is true. If we make it important enough to us it will be important enough to the entire team. Math will reinforce your efforts every time. Get the lifetime value of a client figured out and you'll know how worthwhile this is.

Another way to work on your business and referrals at the same time is in recruiting. Let it be known that you are recruiting top-notch quality employees at all times. Even if you are just starting out I would do this unless you intend to be a solo practitioner forever. By recruiting through referrals early and often you get to tell your story, your hopes, your dreams, and what your company will be in one, three, and five years to very willing listeners. It will give you a queue of people interested in the success of your business and watching how you grow.

While there are many limitations on how you can run a referral reward contest for customers (yes, we reward our customers with prizes for referrals too), in a myriad of industries, hiring bonuses and referral bonuses for employees are most often perfectly acceptable and much, much less expensive than hiring a recruiter. Every time I lose traction on this part I lose momentum when I need to fill a spot in our organization. It's hard to be consistent at executing but incredibly important. We've hired friends, family, sisters, a daughter first and then the mother, customer's children, girlfriends, etc. Because we intentionally try to support employee enrichment we've had multiple people pursue other opportunities and then return to work with us again.

Writing this book has actually gotten us back on track with this element of our business. To watch other people blossom and succeed is a journey that I find incredibly exciting and fulfilling!

# Make it fun

So how do you get people on your team to make referrals a priority? It's a common trap to think of your own industry as boring. You might want to find something else to do if you're falling asleep at your desk out of boredom, but it's pretty common to look at our primary roles as rather mundane.

There's a number of low-cost ways to perk up your team and reinforce the referral reward process you want to promote. Once you've done the math, prizes for referrals can be offered. They can be simple and inexpensive, like candy or other treats, or more lavish, like spa days and trips.

Years ago, when I was still an employee, I designed a contest that the owner signed off on. It included a Caribbean cruise with airfare and the whole nine yards. Not only did it pay big dividends for the agency, a 5-to-1 one-year return on investment and 37.5-to-1 lifetime value return on investment, it was a lovely trip that my wife and I quite enjoyed.

You can engage your team with internal games and activities that don't cost an extraordinary amount of time or money but will grow their loyalty and your company. One of the most effective things is taking games that already exist on TV or in other forms and adjusting them for your own use. "Wheel of Fortune" is one of the most popular game shows of all time. You can buy a real spinning wheel for only a couple of bucks on craigslist.com. Taking that wheel that clickety-clacks and spins around—where-it-stops-nobody-knows—has a powerful effect on team morale because it's just plain fun.

One of the biggest hits we had as an agency was drive-in-movie night. If you still have drive-in movies in your part of the country, try it. It really worked out well and brought the team together. We looked at it as a throwback team-building event that allowed us the chance to spend time together, barbeque, eat junk, stay out late, and take the next day off.

We try to find deposits we can make into our company morale when we want employees to operate slightly outside their comfort zone. It sounds a bit touchy-feely if you're a blood-and-guts numbers achiever, but we're asking them to think about the experience from a customer's perspective.

Here's a list of activities and games we've done over the years to keep it fun, fresh, and lucrative:

- Wheel of Fortune
- Bingo
- Referral prizes for employees
- Gift card drawings
- Pumpkin-carving contest

The fun is not just for employees. Make it fun for your customers. Make sure whatever prizes you give away are memorialized with pictures. Get BIG CHECKS for referral rewards and take pictures of your customers with their prizes. Prominently display referral testimonials in your newsletter and the gratitude for the referrals you've received that month.

for your team, complete with team colors—Gold, Silver, and Bronze medals—the whole works. If they each come up with a team song and motto, all the better.

Outline what you need for referrals to really explode your new business and set that as your goal. Sprinkle in Power Bar breaks, smoothie shake breakfasts, and other assorted Olympic-related events to make it fun and exciting. The duration of the Olympiad should be no more than one month. You want it to be manageable internally from a timeline and to not get stale.

Do the event to coincide with when you most need your pipeline to be crammed full. You might say that's "all the time" but the reality is almost all businesses have an ebb and flow to numbers and prospect meetings. Being in a Midwestern state, our three highest months of reschedules are during the summer. We want to have the pipeline bursting in the late fall/winter, so to keep it topical and fun we make it the Fall Olympics, with hikes to the river for lunch, a scavenger hunt, and maybe even a high-stakes bowling match, with winners getting small prizes.

Our people made up teams with country names with their own colors and flags, and anthems that were played whenever they received a referral. You can adapt it for your organization too. The prizes can be as big or as small as you want.

# Be serious . . . about having fun

One campaign I planned for one of my salespeople had them dressed in different costumes specific to the customer's industry. We scheduled a date, hired a photo crew, set up an industry site location, sent folks out to procure costumes, got an outline of the shots we wanted, and we were all set . . . or so I thought.

Bear in mind, our company was paying for everything, including a planned weekly campaign to support the particular niche we were marketing to. The day before the photo shoot we had to stop and explain to our own team the reason we wanted to be different and have fun with this marketing campaign.

Why couldn't we just send the same kind of marketing material everyone else does? Why would we want to stand out and risk offending someone who doesn't buy from us anywhere (and odds are never will) to attract someone who does like it, remembers it, enjoys it, and does or will buy from us?

Because it works.

People are way, way too serious in business. Be serious about having fun and being memorable and the customers you want will continue to choose you!

Napoleon said, "A soldier will fight long and hard for a bit of colored ribbon." It's true of soldiers and of your employees. Creativity and fun count for much more than money when it comes to internal contests and activities. Everyone wants to belong to something and you can give them that distinction. It seems like a paradox but you need to sell "free" and prizes as much as you would sell something that you charge money for. I know that seems crazy but there is so much noise and static to compete with in today's marketplace, with the added element that people don't actually expect something for nothing. Fun often costs very little but it carries a lot of weight.

Whatever you decide to do, you need to have a well-thought-out and executed plan, whether it's an Office Olympics for your team, a giveaway event for customers, or selling a million-dollar product.

Having fun can be hard work, especially when you are organizing the fun for others. The key is repeated communication of when, what to expect, testimonials supporting the event, and a big payoff. It doesn't have to be in monetary value but it does need to be in perceived value. An audience with a celebrity, a glimpse at something secret, a pampering that's unusual, a contest, a chance to laugh from the belly, etc., are only some of myriad ways you can find to make it fun if you'll let yourself. If it doesn't work the first or second time, keep at it; you'll be repaid in kind.

Referral marketing is a family affair for me. My brother Doug hired me in my wayward youth to work for him in his print shop/marketing company. Shortly after, he joined a breakfast networking group and came back with stories of business and referrals to work on. Though he is by far one of the best natural networkers I've ever met in my life, his referral marketing wasn't really honed or turned into a system until much later.

Doug got bored with the printing business and its commodity shopping mentality and decided to narrow his focus to a seasonal business. He had moved to San Diego about ten years earlier and realized that people really missed their hometowns, especially around the holidays, so he opened a Christmas tree lot about two blocks from the beach. Huh? His friends and, okay maybe our family said, "You really think a Christmas tree lot is going to make money at the beach?"

Well, it turned out that yes, indeed, when people were feeling homesick, a little, or even a bigger, tree made them feel much better around the holidays. It turned out you can also charge a wee bit more in San Diego for a Christmas tree than, say, Minneapolis.

As other industrious folks watched and saw the success of the little lot by the beach, they decided some competition was in order.

Doug's next step was to deliver an entire experience at his lot as the competitors came up with "cheaper" prices. Hot cider, candy canes, Santa Claus—all the accessories to create a reason for families to hang out at his business.

Then he gave a photo, a Polaroid in those days, and added a friends-and-family discount for everyone who signed up for his mailing list, promising to deliver next year's flyer to them as well and "allowed" them to invite other family members to use the same discount if they brought them along.

This worked really well for a couple of years but the competitors kept coming so Doug added another wrinkle. He opened the Pumpkin Patch in October to ramp up the season. The Pumpkin Patch was a much lower risk/lower reward proposition than the Christmas tree lot but it became a referral machine.

By inviting area businesses to give away free Halloween spider rings in a plastic pumpkin on their counters, he was able to distribute an invitation to the Pumpkin Patch for an incredibly low cost. This allowed him to give the business a discount on a tree for their office and for all of the employees they referred to the Christmas tree lot.

Of course everyone who came to the Pumpkin Patch also received an opportunity to refer their family and friends to the "special family discount" on Christmas trees. This has served to keep competitors at bay for years and secure the loyalty of "family and friends" to his lot like no other.

# Freshen it up!!

In particular, if you have short-term recognition, you can try the newest gadget, gizmo, or trend-setting item to freshen up your reward program. One item we used frequently a few years ago were FLIP videos. They were really cool, most people didn't have them, and most importantly, when we delivered them we could show how they worked and get a video testimonial. Originally, we added the video testimonials to our website, which was kind of cool at the time because not that many people were doing it. Then we really freshened it up and created a video testimonial library on our iPad presentations. This turned out to be a move that created something very new for our prospects and clients, led to a much higher conversion percentage, and increased our retention.

We like to take the basics of marketing and relationships and just reshape them slightly. Another example is video emails. Two companies we've used are Vidbiscuit <http://vidbiscuit.com/> and NetBriefings <http://www.netbriefings.com/>. Both are good and both can do the job. I'm sure there are other similar technologies to test. We don't send video email to anyone we are not in a relationship with. We use it to support our referral, marketing, relationship, and customer on-boarding process. It's important to support this with other forms of media for the best results. The technology tracks how many of them get opened and watched.

Voice broadcasting is a tool we use solely for nurturing and client appreciation events. It allows us to contact all of our customers with one recorded call on timely events or seasonal nurturing messages. I don't think it's a great attraction medium, but in our case it's a good way to get the message to our customers to watch out for the kids and drive safely on Halloween. We allow our nonprofits to use our line for charity and community events. When we are going to do something, for instance our shredding event, it's a great way to support other media.

I did get a little crazy one year and gave away a car for a referral reward prize. In fact, that's the actual car on the cover of the book; the woman who won it was more than happy to let us use it for the cover. She keeps it stored all winter long so it will look eye-popping sharp in the summer.

People definitely thought I was nuts but since I knew our math, I wasn't too concerned about it paying off. I must admit that with the deafening roar of "How can you do that?!!" I did check my math on multiple occasions. A little caution here: Make sure you check your local and state laws about prize giveaways and the correct steps needed to keep it legal. You don't want to have a wonderful opportunity become a nightmare scenario due to litigation or censure. The laws are different state by state and industry by industry.

What we learned most from doing this huge giveaway was that we didn't materially increase our results by increasing our grand prize value 30 times. The important thing is that we continue our reward process and focus on communicating it to our team, customers, prospects, and circle of influences consistently and with multiple media.

## THE BEST REFERRAL OF MY LIFE

Early in my career, I received the best referral of my entire life. My neighbors, Keith and Abby Mackey, wanted me to meet someone Abby worked with, a lovely woman named Cindy. They thought we would be a good fit. At a minimum, she was awesome and I wasn't a murderer.

We went with the Mackeys for Sunday brunch and a Twins game and the rest is, as they say . . . Actually, the history is still being written. Cindy and I have been married over twenty years and have two beautiful children, Patrick and Colleen (you may have noticed her in that cool car on the cover). That's been the best math and multiplier from any referral I've ever received.

# Newsletters

Don't forget public acknowledgment. Spotlight a customer each month in your newsletter, either something interesting that one of your customers does personally or about his or her business.

Throw away the canned newsletter and take the time to let your personality through. If your customers truly feel they know you, it will be harder for them to ever leave. Even if you need the structure provided by a canned published newsletter, get one in which you can claim authorship of the articles and edit them to take away any staleness. Make them sound like you. People will start to see your personality come through and it will build your relationship.

In today's day and age of elance.com, the Professional Editors Network (www.pensite.org), and other writing sources that you can connect with for very affordable prices, there is no way you shouldn't make an effort to personalize your newsletter to let your customers know you and your company. The more they know you and like you, the less likely they will ever leave.

# Make it transferable

When our company takes on a new customer, one of our checklist items is to ask them how they create sales. Who are their customers and where do they come from? What do they do to encourage referrals?

It gives us an opportunity to introduce our referral program, to discuss at length how it helps us grow, the industry average for the length of time that people remain clients, our average, and most importantly, *their* business model for growth and success. Explaining our business and giving them a look behind the curtain (something nobody has ever explained to them before) opens a dialogue of trust and communication that often isn't possible otherwise. It also creates an open discussion that allows us to help them succeed or, at a minimum, to let them know that we'll do all we can to help them succeed.

Use your marketing skills (and the ones you learn from this book) to help your customers develop their own referral reward program.

I will admit that I have always found this far simpler than our sales team. I've discovered over the years that this is definitely not Sales 101. I'm not sure if it's graduate level or not, but be prepared for three things:

1. It will take a considerable amount of time, training, and follow-up with your sales team to have them effectively execute this strategy.

2. The salespeople you take the time to train will get more referrals than ever before.

3. Customers you effectively execute this strategy with will be customers for life.

I can say Number 3 emphatically from our own experience. Our industry average for length of customer relationship is 7.5 years. Our Top 50 customers have been with us an average of 19 years and most of them are in concert with us in helping one another succeed. We spend more time talking about how we can successfully utilize each other's systems than anything else we do. One of our key customers said it best: "Shaun, I consider you part of *our* team. You are consistently helping us to be successful and grow. You anticipate our needs because you know what's going on with us and know us so well."

Getting long-term profitable and successful customers means long-term success for you and your organization but it leads you to completely different conversations with your customers that often have nothing to do with the product or service you provide them.

Recently, one of our clients, who had a well-thought-out idea of who his ideal client is, was lamenting his inability to find someone to set the table for identifying those prospective customers. It was exciting to hear how they determined the ideal customer and other factors—how many employees they would need, distance to parking availability, ability to do a payroll deduction pre-tax for transportation costs, etc. That alone was incredibly worthwhile for me as a business owner. But even better, because of the discussion, I had a way I could help them.

One of our offices is located just a few blocks from a major university with 30,000 students. We have a research assistant and what our customer was describing seemed perfectly aligned with the interests of our student employee. We set up a lunch to get the table set and within a month the research was done and delivered to our client for next to nothing. This story may seem to be a tangent that has nothing to do with making your referral process transferable but it's entirely part of the process.

Understanding how your customers succeed and produce sales will bring you closer to them. If you do this well, and listen with an open mind, you'll also be able to add some of their methods to your current attraction, conversion, and retention processes.

The often reported mantra of "Our business is different" is a tired cliché and an excuse for the laziness of not wanting to do the work, the stubbornness of thinking your own way is the only way, and a lack of creativity to incorporate other people's ideas and processes with your own for even greater success. Clearly delineated steps in your referral process will enable you to describe it better for your team and your customers and transfer it to them.

Every businessperson you meet can add value to your referral system. Start an idea folder. Ask yourself:

Do the businesses you deal with rely on big referrals or multiple small ones?

Where do they get the bulk of their new business sales?

Who are their circles of influence?

Do they ask their customers how *they* succeed?

What's the timeline from referral to adding that referral as a customer?

What's the payoff or expected lifetime value of each client relationship for them?

How often do clients use them once they are hired?

Questions like these will help you to understand your customers' businesses and help them adopt some form of your own referral program for their success.

The more you listen the more you can take pieces of their success template and incorporate them into your own business and multiply your success. Make sure they know it if you add an element of their program to yours. Imitation is the sincerest form of flattery. I guarantee if you have a "marketing" session with your key clients, your relationship will last longer and will be more fruitful and open than any transactional relationships you have.

Business owners and leaders too often feel that nobody cares about their business and success. It can be very lonely. Business owners can't share everything with their employees because they need to confidently forge ahead but more often than not, when I've gotten a CEO comfortable enough to open up, I found a man or woman who welcomed having the ear of someone "safe" to discuss things with.

# Track It

What gets measured gets done! I don't know who gets the credit for having said it first, but I know it to be true. Businesses ultimately function on people executing steps and processes that will be measured by someone responsible for incorporating them into a financial statement, be that a customer or a boss. The mission and vision of an organization are attracted to ideals and the framework of specific ways of doing business. Marketing and sales that have been proven to be effective are measured. They are measured by campaign, return on investment, media, lifetime value of a customer, and any other number of ways that will give you the capability to respect whatever is working to gain your ideal customer and to quit doing what's not working.

Years ago we decided to do a Yellow Pages ad. It seems kind of quaint now with the massive changes in media and our culture, but at the time the Yellow Pages was a viable marketing medium and strategy if used properly, with an ad that could stand out and results that could be measured.

We wrote excellent copy, negotiated for very good page-placement, assigned and bought tracking numbers, and absolutely had the phones ringing off the hook. Sounds fantastic, doesn't it? But we had more than a little problem: we were getting the wrong type of customer calling us. We were attracting an extraordinary number of phone calls for the cost of the ad but not the right market segment. It was a lot like running an ad for ketchup when you really sell salsa. They're both red, and both are condiments (the Number 1 condiment in America, in fact, is salsa), but not the same thing. Worse yet, as we continued to track it and the amount of time we spent explaining that we sell salsa, not ketchup, the results were worse. We managed to light up the phones with over 425 prospect calls per month, of which fewer than 20 fit our ideal client criteria. Oops, it happens. But you wouldn't know it or, potentially, correct it if you weren't tracking it properly.

Referrals, on the other hand, are so extraordinarily powerful and profitable they will bring nothing but smiles to your face if you track them. We consistently have 5 to 15-to-1 returns in the first revenue year, year in and year out. As we grow, our new average client value has been even more interesting. When you multiply lifetime value for clients, 7.5 for us times annual revenue, it is 75 to 1.

Digging deeper into your tracking will also help you to know which referral relationships to foster and how. A good friend of mine, Jacques Gibbs, an awesome relationship developer, had a tracking system to referral conduits. Whether they were customers or other professionals he learned, and remembered, their ages, common interests, any overlap of customer segments, and even religion.

His theory was that if you could hit four out of seven similarities or, better yet, passions, you'd be well on your way to building a meaningful relationship. It worked well for him and finding common interests with people suited his personality to a "T."

Jacques kept it simple when describing what it took to be successful in referrals:

- Show up on time.
- Do what you say you're going to do.
- Finish what you start.
- Say "Please" and "Thank you."
- Repeat steps one through four.

# Tracking isn't hard

You don't need special software or an elaborate tracking program. We use a simple spreadsheet with the following categories.

Number
Drawing Month
Referral Reward Sent
Referring Party Name
Referring Party Company
Address
City
State
ZIP
Referred Individual/ Contact
Referred Company
Tracking
Change Date
Producer
CSR/ Employee
Account Type
Account Notation
Status
Date of Referral
Date Quoted
Date Written
Est. Revenue
Reason Not Written
Charity
Notes

# Do it again if it worked

Throughout the last ten years of my career I've been part of a national marketing group that gets together once per quarter. We learn a lot from each other and inevitably have a laugh over a common theme. Someone will mention a campaign that worked well for his company in years gone by, or just in the last year, and someone else will ask, "Why did you quit doing it?"

"Well, we got busy!" is usually the answer.

So let me get this straight: It worked really well, the phones rang, you sold lots of stuff, so you quit doing it. The point is twofold. Marketing, sales, and creative types love the new shiny idea, thing, niche, etc., and I already fell on the sword regarding this with recruiting when I shared that we've gone through periods when we did this really well and then, lo and behold, "we got busy." So mea culpa.

Another thing I realized in writing, editing, and getting excited about sharing these ideas and principles with you is that we can do so much better than we've done in the last couple of years. Don't get me wrong; we're fortunate to have a very robust practice and great customers but small steps to tweak it will bring us more wonderful relationships and people. In getting this down on paper I've developed a commitment to triple our referrals. The way I'll personally do it is to give three referrals per week because I know it will lead to lifting other people who will in turn lift us.

Before embarking on a new campaign, take the time to review previous successful campaigns to see if they can be restarted, with or without changes. If you've tracked results, you should be able to get it back up and running very quickly for a shorter timeline on ROI. Ask what part of the process bogged down the continued execution of leads. Is it fixed? Is it worth fixing? Are the customers you brought into the fold still the ideal customer candidates for your continued growth? All of these should be straightforward questions easily answered if you've tracked well.

The second part of the review can assess what parts of other campaigns can be replicated for the new and improved plan. It's simply more efficient when you know that one element worked really well with your target audience to use it again. I've found over the course of running campaigns that the default for marketing people is to look at each one in a vacuum and not take the lessons we learned from tracking the prior campaigns. They don't always look for the shortcuts to success that we need to boost our profits and get it out the door. In their defense, if we don't know what works in our businesses and don't track our campaigns, it's our own dumb fault. **Tracking can seem boring if you only focus on the mechanics of it, not the results.**

The strategic plan is fueled by dreams but executed by the tactics and mechanics of tracking. All the higher-level aspirations you have in your sights will be accomplished more fully and completely by tracking. Track and celebrate!

# Give It Away
## (It always comes back)

There are countless phrases that sum up the law of reciprocity: What goes around comes around; Karma; the rubber band (a TV show called "Becker" had a really funny episode on this); invite the best.

They're not just phrases; it's true. We have every reason to be grateful and help others, not only because it's the right thing to do, but you can do so fearlessly because it will return to you in kind. It's happened countless times to me in practice but you don't need to believe me to know it's true. Try it on for size or think back to the times you've given selflessly.

The pursuit of money isn't enough for many of us because we understand the gifts we've been given by others. Giving away your "secrets" is a testament to how many people have taught you over the years. Giving away your time and money is simply the right thing to do.

It's been said that finding the big-enough reason lifts all barriers in getting things done. We hear it time after time in immigrants' stories around the world, people who work two or three jobs to send money home; people who have scrimped and saved and lived together so they could bring their families to America, Europe, or wherever.

When I was a young college student I met a man, Luc, from the Philippines. He worked at night cleaning the building where I was a computer operator. He was a friendly guy and we chatted quite a few times. I learned he was a college-educated engineer who had made it to America nine years earlier. There had been, and continued to be, political upheaval in his native Philippines so he wanted a better life for his family. His solution was to forgo his professional career, come to America and work three jobs, none of them anywhere near the money his education or training warranted, and send that money home so his siblings could come, one by one, to America with their families.

He didn't share his story with me for a pity-party, mostly it came in bits and pieces as I got to know him better. He believed that America gave him so much by giving him his freedom that he desperately wanted to give it to everyone in his family. It affected me deeply, that the gift of freedom was so monumental that he was compelled to give it to others.

All of our treasures, most of all our freedom, have been given to us by someone else.

Certainly we don't attain any financial, emotional, or spiritual well-being without the help of too many people to ever count. Find what you value most and find a way to give it away. Teach, volunteer, write checks, share your passion—all of them will multiply the well-being of others and you, more than you will ever know.

"Give it away" sounds revolutionary until you sit down a year after sharing your entire marketing strategy with someone who loved it, related to it, and had every intention of implementing it but you find out they didn't. You could give away your entire business plan and strategy to your competitors every year and 99% of them wouldn't do a thing with it. The 1% would normally be willing to tell you what's working for them and be the better for it as well. Giving it away to your customers just stands to build goodwill and more successful relationships.

It's extremely gratifying to see what you've given work for someone else. A local nonprofit we support, the Cookie Cart, www.cookiecart.org, gives inner-city teens, ages 14–17, their first paid job experiences and training through a commercial/referral bakery. To most people it sounds odd that this would be a critical need because they have parents to shepherd them and teach them, but too many of these youngsters have never, or rarely, had someone leave for work every morning to show them the way through modeling a work ethic.

So many things that we might take for granted due to our upbringing—good health, proximity to excellent transportation, or education—are not part of a growing number of people's experiences in their formative years. You can give your abundant energy, talent, or money to organizations or people for research into diseases near and dear to your heart, or to help folks, for example, with developmental disabilities, who will never have the capacity to be in highly functioning intellectual positions but nonetheless deserve our best efforts to respectfully address their wants, needs, and their shot at a relatively full life.

A dear friend, mentor, and successful business leader, Bob Klas, one of the founders of the Tapemark Charity Pro-Am golf tournament, likes to tell me that even when people give selfishly they realize just how good it feels to do good for others.

Two families decided over forty years ago to do something to help people with developmental disabilities. They started modestly with fairly limited goals to help folks with developmental disabilities get a better shake in the world.

Think of the context of those times. The government had recently deinstitutionalized thousands of people with developmental disabilities after counseling parents for decades that the best place for their children with developmental disabilities was in government-run or privately run institutions where they could be with people "like them." That turned out to be a monumental failure and when the government undid it and sent these folks out into the world, there were few support structures or mechanisms in place for dealing with even their basic needs. As often happens, the ripple effect and unintended consequences continue to be felt over 45 years later.

The Tapemark Charity Pro-Am has raised over $6.5 million in the last forty years for nonprofit agencies serving Minnesota children and adults living with developmental disabilities and their families. It has grown to be recognized as a distinctive signature charitable golf event for the Midwest. Seeking to give it away in a small way grew and multiplied into an event impacting thousands of lives.

Your impact can be similarly felt by more people than you will ever know. Find something that interests you or moves your heart and you will be amazed at what you can give away.

# Why/Who?

To receive a great number of referrals you need to think of helping others and consistently refer business to other professionals, the key being to refer to other professionals who you know, either through your own experience or on good authority. You will do an amazing job for the people you want to help. Your reputation depends on it. I had a referral once that ended very badly for the person I referred. The person I referred them to completely dropped the ball in communication and execution, a double whammy. It taught me a lesson. It wasn't not to refer people; it was to know exactly what kind of professional I was referring people to, preferably through my own experience, but short of that, through the experience of people I know and trust.

It's not enough to have someone tell you they are good at something or to rely on a slick website. We added a three-years-in-business guideline to one of the networking groups I attended to weed out people in our peer group who were still trying to find their careers, who were not yet ready for prime time. We wanted people who were going to be there for the duration if we were going to refer them to our most valued clients.

Another very clear set of rules I live by is to follow up with the person I give a referral to. It does a couple of things. It lets me know whether the person who has received the referral followed up with them and helped them solve their situation, and it reinforces that I care about helping them. Your friends and/or associates don't always want to tell you if a referral doesn't work out. Be thoughtful and follow up yourself so they don't have to. It will make you look good, help them to get a better outcome, and it will get you more referrals.

From this interaction you'll also be able to figure out whether they will be a AAA referral source. You'll find that the more willing they are to interact about the referral, the process, and how they do it will be a solid indicator of their emotions regarding referrals. If you run into people who have an inflated sense of the value of the one referral they give but don't seem to remember the referrals they get, it will be readily apparent they won't be a good referral relationship.

# REFERRALS—WHY— REFERRALS—WHY— REFERRALS—WHY?

Referrals are bringing someone you care about to someone you trust. Don't ever forget that element of it and you'll forever be successful at it. "Referral worshiper" is a description I can live with. So is evangelist. If you care about people you'll care deeply about positive outcomes.

I have forgotten this over the years on multiple occasions and it breaks my heart when I get it wrong. It takes no longer to do something right than worry about how you goofed it up.

# CONVERSION —
## IT HAPPENS EVERY TIME

The very best way to convert every referral is to go back to Jacques' maxim:

> Show up on time!
> Do what you say you're going to do!
> Finish what you start!
> Say "Please" and "Thank You!"

If you fully concentrate on helping the person who is calling you to solve their problem or get them on the path to solving their situation, you've converted the referral for good. This might sound too soft for you, not hard-boiled-business enough for you, and too simplistic. Remember, I started with nothing, actually less than nothing because I owed money. Referrals have meant multi-millions to our business. I know it works and I know it will work for you too. It's difficult only in that you have to listen, care, and be genuine in trying to help them.

The noise of the world and the chaos surrounding us have people craving a real connection, someone who will slow down and listen, who they know hears them and cares, and who they know will be there the next time they need them. That doesn't mean that if you can't do it, you should just blow them off and move on. It means listening intently and thinking about what help would you want if you were in their situation, and asking yourself if you know how to find it for them. More times than not you'll be able to move them forward on the path to the solution, whether it's you or not.

The magic comes in communicating your results to the person who referred them and then repeating it over and over and over until you convince yourself that it's a phenomenal way to build a remarkable business made up of friends who think just like you.

# Acknowledgments

My mother says I was born a salesman. Maybe she's right. I'm not so sure about that nature/nurture business anyway, but I do know this: she showed us how to give when we had what would appear, to the naked eye, as very little.

She taught us how to give generously of our time, energy, and spirit for things that we cared about, or to help others fuel their passions.

That's continued in my work life with great people like Lee Lauer, my first boss at Anderson Agency; Mark Kraemer, who walked away from the company he owned and continues to believe in me every day; Bob and Sandy Klas, Bob Klas, Jr., Tom Cody, and their entire families who have dedicated their time and resources to giving back. This led to me joining City of Lakes Rotary, where I've seen Service Above Self in action that is literally mind-boggling—people lifting up people in their city and half a world away through vision, enthusiasm, and united energy for doing good work.

I hope I've given you a template to find the same, or better yet, more success than we've been able to build. It's amazing to me every day how fortunate we are.

## SHAUN IRWIN

is president of Anderson Agency, a Minneapolis-based independent insurance agency. His rags-to-riches story is as literal as they come: simply in need of a job to feed his family, he started as the agency mail clerk. Eleven years later . . . fueled by luck, love, friendship, learning, gratitude and the power of referral-based growth . . . he bought the agency.

A nationally recognized author, speaker, consultant, and consumer advocate, Shaun actively participates in and supports a variety of community and civic organizations. He lives near Minneapolis with his wife and two children.

You can reach Shaun with your success stories, for speaking engagements, or order more books at www.convertiblereferrals.com or Shaunirwin.com.